DINOSAUR DIG!

Triceratops

Allosaurus

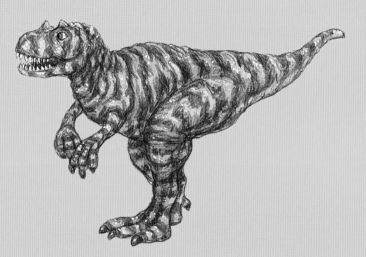

Iguanodon

Ankylosaurus

Deinonychus

Megalosaurus

Stegosaurus

Baryonyx

Styracosaurus

Tyrannosaurus rex

For Zachary

First published 2011 by Nosy Crow Ltd
The Crow's Nest, 10a Lant Street
London SE1 1QR
www.nosycrow.com

ISBN 978 0 85763 094 0 (PB)

A CIP catalogue record for this book is available from the British Library.

Printed in China

DINOSAUR DIG!

Penny Dale

nosy crow

One dinosaur digging, digging a hole.

Two dinosaurs shovelling,
shovelling gravel and earth.

Tons of gravel
and earth.

Clatter!

Clatter!

Three dinosaurs **tipping,** tipping dirt and **rock.**

Dirt and rock, tumbling down.

Crash!

Crash!

Crash!

Four dinosaurs lifting, lifting massive blocks of stone.

Blocks of stone,
shaking the ground.

Thump!

Thump!

Thump!

Five dinosaurs mixing, mixing sticky **cement.**

Sticky cement on shiny trowels.

Six dinosaurs building, building up and up.

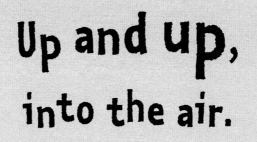

Up and up,
into the air.

Clunk!

Clunk!

Clunk!

Seven dinosaurs rolling,
rolling grit and sand.
Grit and sand, flat and smooth.

Eight dinosaurs **pumping,**
pumping lumpy **concrete.**
Concrete **squirts** from giant pipes.

Sploosh!

Sploosh!

Nine dinosaurs **spraying,** spraying bright blue **paint.**

Ten dinosaurs waiting...

watching and waiting...

Getting ready...

getting ready to make a **BIG**...

Splash!

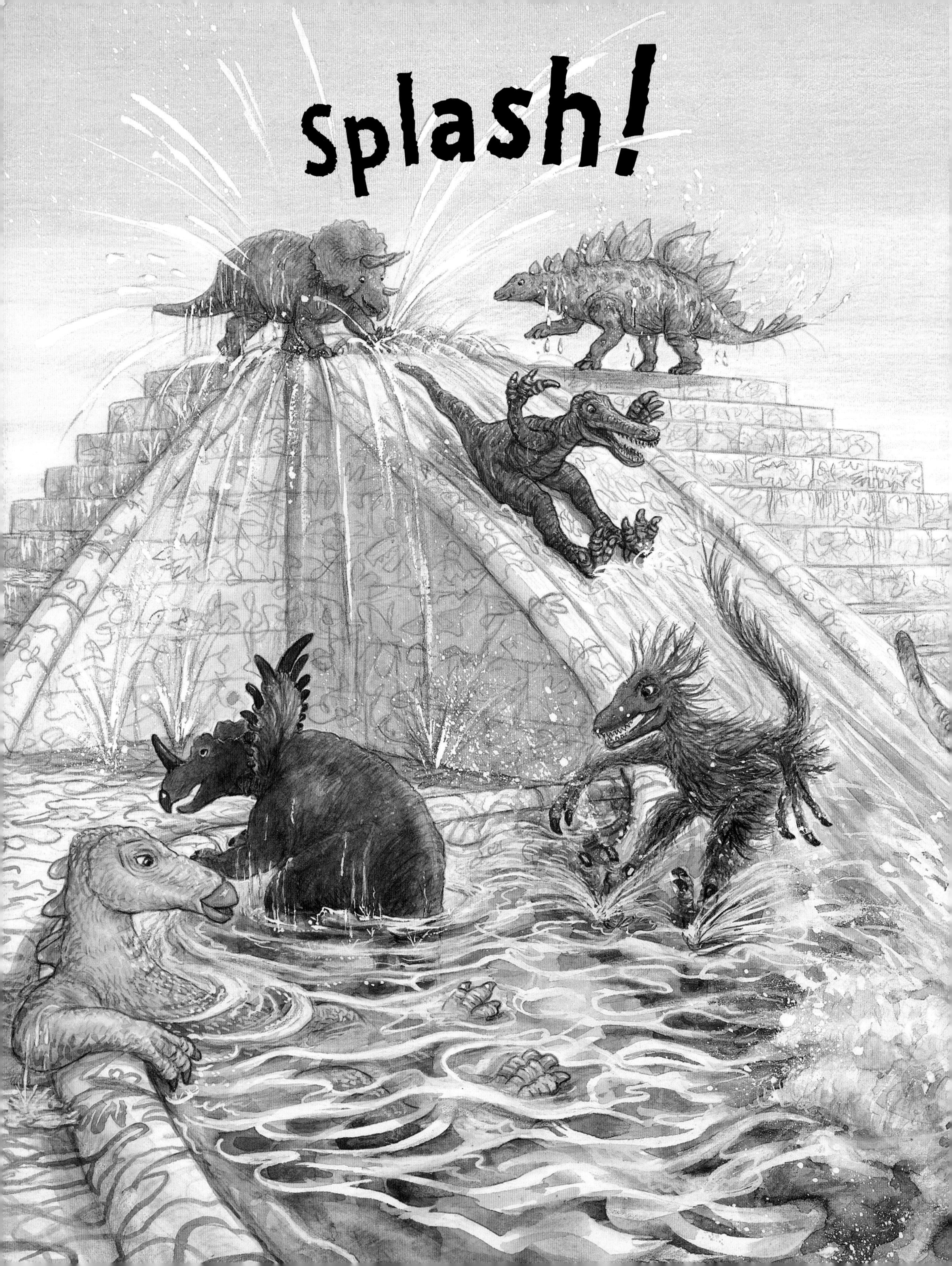

Loader

Telehandler

Roller

Truck
Crane

Paint Truck

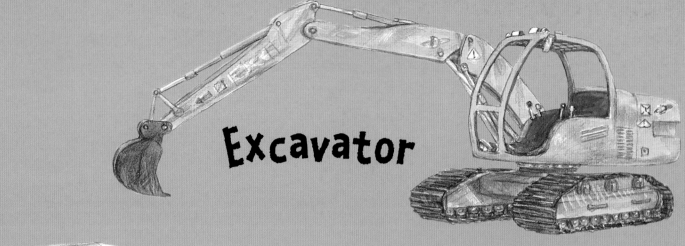

Excavator

Concrete Pumper

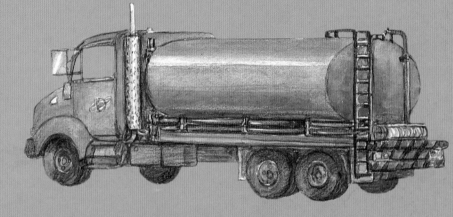

Truck and Mixer

Water Tanker

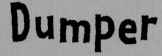

Dumper